Simply Faithful
My Catholic Prayer Journal

Our Lady of Lourdes

Our Sunday Visitor
Huntington, Indiana

Our Sunday Visitor Publishing Division
Our Sunday Visitor, Inc.
200 Noll Plaza
Huntington, IN 46750
1-800-348-2440

ISBN: 978-1-68192-951-4 (Inventory No. T2686)

LCCN: 2021935515

Reflections and prayer prompts written by Barb Szyszkiewicz
Cover and interior art: Abigail Halpin
Cover and interior design: Tyler Ottinger

PRINTED IN THE UNITED STATES OF AMERICA

Prayer is our way of communicating with God. We read in the Gospels that Jesus modeled prayer by going off by himself to pray, and he even taught us a specific way to pray in the prayer we now know as the Our Father, or the Lord's Prayer.

We can connect with God in praise and thanksgiving. We can also express remorse for our sins and go to God with our own needs and those of others.

Sometimes when we pray, words don't come easily, and it can help to write out our thoughts. Keeping a prayer journal allows you to chronicle your communication with God. You don't pray the same way every time, and you don't have to use your prayer journal the same way every time.

Ten ways you can use a prayer journal:

1. Compose your own prayers.
2. List special prayer intentions.
3. Count your blessings: Take note of answered prayers.
4. Begin the day by listing three ways you hope God will bless the day.
5. End the day with an examination of conscience.
6. Record your thoughts while reading the Bible; the day's Mass readings are a great place to start.
7. Write down your favorite prayers, Bible verses, or hymn lyrics that inspire you to pray.
8. Paste in some holy cards or photos of loved ones you want to keep in prayer.
9. Jot down homily notes.
10. Write a letter to God or to a saint.

Praying with Our Lady of Lourdes

In February 1858, an uneducated teenage girl gathering firewood with her friends near Lourdes, France, suddenly stopped everything when she saw a beautiful lady above a small grotto where animals often sheltered. This began a series of eighteen apparitions of the Blessed Mother to a site that has come to earn a reputation for healings, both physical and spiritual.

Young Bernadette Soubirous, who at age thirteen had not yet made her first Communion, and who could not read or write, experienced Our Lady of Lourdes as a kind, gentle, and motherly presence.

What spiritual lessons can we learn from the story of Our Lady of Lourdes?

Invitation: At their first meeting, the Blessed Mother invited Bernadette to come closer. Later, Bernadette felt drawn to return to the grotto, even when her family and the local authorities tried to prevent her from going there.

Humility: Without a formal education, Bernadette was not cynical or jaded. She was not concerned about how she appeared to her family or her neighbors. She accepted the gift of the visits from the Blessed Mother and sought to carry out Our Lady's wishes.

Kindness: Our Lady spoke to Bernadette in her own dialect and even asked if Bernadette would be so kind as to visit her at the grotto for fifteen days. The Blessed Mother was a model of kindness to a child who knew very little of that in her life.

Trust: Bernadette, trusting that Our Lady was good, was receptive to hearing her messages.

As you journal, explore how these themes are reflected in your spiritual life.

Our Lady of Lourdes signaled to Bernadette to come closer. How can I draw closer to Mary today?

Our Lady told Bernadette, "I do not come to make you happy in this world, but in the next." Am I humble enough to seek happiness in God alone?

Do I reach out to
others in kindness,
without self-interest?
What kindness can
I show to someone
today?

How am I called to
trust God today?